Seven Steps to Effective Prayer

An Instruction Book for Affirmative Prayer

by Peter C. Gray

This book is not intended as a substitute for medical advice or treatment. If you need medical advice or treatment, see a qualified medical doctor. Neither the author nor publisher is responsible for any adverse effects of your use or misuse of the techniques or information presented herein.

CAMPBELL BOOKS
A division of Rainbow Marketing
PO Box 522
Rockaway, NJ 07866

ISBN 0-9720187-0-0
Printed in the United States of America
2 4 6 8 10 9 7 5 3 1

Dedicated to Dr. Peggy Basset who taught me Affirmative Prayer and showed me how to change my life.

Also dedicated to those who are seeking. May these words assist you on your path to realize that all of your answers are within.

Seven Steps to Effective Prayer

An Instruction Book for Affirmative Prayer

by Peter C. Gray

TABLE OF CONTENTS

Acknowledgements

I acknowledge with extreme gratitude a vast number of teachers and colleagues who have assisted me along the way. I would not venture to name them all.

There are several who deserve special recognition:
Barbara Hart, writer, editor, publisher, who told me that I could write and dared to publish some of my early poems and essays.

John Hannes, who provided a period of stability and encouragement that enabled me to complete the book.

Shirley Miller, an extraordinary editor, who ripped the book apart and had me put it together in a more coherent form. This is a better book because of her work.

Michelle Wadleigh for her prayer work to support the book.

To the following for providing financial sponsorship for the printing costs: Stephen Bartlett, Janice Billera, Steve and Margaret Corsello, Eileen Foley, John Hannes, Jerri Judick, Joe and Trina Lavinia,

All mistakes, errors, mis-communications and failures are mine alone. I would appreciate any feedback that is warranted. I can be reached at: petegray@inpro.net.

Dear Reader,

This book is designed to teach you how to write prayers that can change your life. The method used, which is called Affirmative Prayer or Spiritual Mind Treatment is an easy to learn structure used to build your own unique prayer.

It does not matter whether or not you are affiliated with any church, synagogue, or temple. It does not even matter if you subscribe to any religious philosophy. If you have an understanding that there is a Higher Power, a spiritual energy in the universe, you can use this prayer technique to improve your conditions. If you are involved in any organized religion, this method will not interfere with anything that you have been taught. Although most religions have prayer books to read or memorize, very few actually teach a method of creating a prayer that is specific to your needs and desires.

I did not invent the methods taught here. They have been tried and proven over many years. I learned them during four years of training and the subsequent five years of work as a licensed practitioner in a Science of Mind Center. Many of the examples given here come from that experience. Where any name is used, it has been changed to protect the confidentiality of the persons involved.

Welcome to an exciting adventure.

Pete Gray
Morristown, New Jersey

CHAPTER ONE

PRAYER

The power of prayer is not a new idea. Legend tells us that ancient nomadic hunters prayed for a successful hunt. Early planters prayed for the proper amounts of sunshine and rain for a bountiful harvest. Early man understood the concept of a power greater than himself. However, he did not understand the phenomenon of nature. Knowing weather could not be controlled, he prayed to nature's gods to invoke the proper conditions for growth of their grains. Over a period of time family groups began to cluster together to share their labor. They created more gods. Among them was a god of fertility to increase the size of the tribe, a god of war for victory in battle, a god of love for companionship.

It became apparent that some prayers proved more effective than others. Sometimes a prayer got the desired results. Sometimes it did not. Many things were tried to render prayer more effective. Complicated, involved and sometimes torturous rituals were instituted. Sacrifices of plants, animals and even humans were made. Music was added to enhance prayer. Dance forms, some long and exhausting, were created. Memory aids and counting devices such as beads, feathers, bones, or shells were added. Symbols such as dolls, masks, totems, carvings were devised. Statues, paintings, and other images of gods, saints, or symbols developed. Certain individuals seemed to have more talent than others in speaking their word and manifesting the desired effects. These people evolved into Shaman, Guru, Witch Doctor, Priest or Priestess.

Rituals, symbols and dances combined with prayer were attempts to increase the realization of the desired result. Why do some prayers seem to be more effective than others? Why do some people seem more able to manifest the effects they desire? What can we do to increase the demonstrations resulting from our own? That is the purpose of this book.

Although I use the word "God" throughout this book, there are other names used to identify a higher power. My early religious training taught me that god was a judge and I was most likely condemned. As a young man I rejected the "God as judge" idea and all religions with it. However, I still recognized a higher power, a guiding force in the universe. It did not seem possible to me that the construction of the universe from the largest galaxy to the smallest atom could have happened by chance. I could not accept that the evolutionary process of life on earth from the first amoeba to the intelligence of humankind was pure accident.

An article on the Big Bang theory of evolution in the June 1983 issue of National Geographic magazine contains the sentence, "[The universe] began with an incredibly tiny, intensely energized speck." That article went on to explain the current scientific thinking on the beginnings of the universe. It said that everything: galaxies and stars, solar systems and planets, oceans and mountains, plants and animals, the race of humankind, you, me, everything, evolved from that "intensely energized speck." There was nothing that existed before except that energy.

The Bible begins with the words "In the beginning God..." I have come to believe that in the beginning there was God, and nothing else. That everything: galaxies and stars, you and me, and everything else, evolved from and is an expression of that "intensely energized force." I believe that each individual is a part of that unfathomable enormity that we call God. That God is within each of us. That God is not "out there" someplace. God is not in a heaven, not sitting on a throne making judgments, not in a church or synagogue. God is right here. God is inside me. In my computer, the lamp that lights the room, the maple tree outside the window, the birds singing in its branches. God is within you, the ones you love, and the ones you do not. God is everything. Everything is God. *"There is one God, the Father, from whom comes everything and by whom we live."* (I Corinthians 8:6.)

When I first began to learn the method of prayer described here, I could not use the word "God." If this is true for you, then find a word that is more comfortable. It is sometimes easier to refer to Higher Power, Spirit, Source, Energy, Mother Earth, Nature, Law, Love, Christ, or some other term that symbolizes for you a loving, caring God.

Mind

One of the names I like for God is Universal Mind. I believe that the mind of each individual is a part of that Universal Mind. Our individual mind is the part of us with which we think. Universal Mind is the point in God Consciousness where we are connected at all times with the Higher Power. This point of contact allows us to communicate with the Higher Power.

In his book, *The Dancing Wu Li Masters,* physicist Gary Zukav explains quantum physics simply and clearly. He shows that the expectation and attitude of the scientist performing quantum experiments, affect the results of those experiments. So our attitudes, beliefs and expectations affect the results in our lives. Old attitudes, old beliefs can be changed. We choose each day, whether to keep old beliefs or change them. As we change our beliefs, the results in our lives change. The form of prayer used here is called Spiritual Mind Treatment. It is a technique, a method of re-choosing, and a way to change those deeply rooted beliefs.

Mind is a concept, an idea, not a place. There is no part of the body that I can touch and say, "This is my mind." There is no part of the brain that a physician can point to as the mind. Mind is the invisible atmosphere in, through, and surrounding our visible bodies. There are two categories of mind, the objective (or conscious), and the subjective (or subconscious). The objective mind is the part of us that thinks, that has choice that can make decisions. The subjective is the creative part of mind that is "subject to" the thoughts of objective mind. It is also the home of memory and our belief systems.

The subjective is the area of mind where man and God are united, where all humans and all things are connected. It is the atmosphere of our beliefs, the state where memory is stored, and the place where we retain the meaning of our experiences. Books have been published about extra sensory perception, the mental phenomena where one person can understand the thoughts of another. Many of us have experienced this phenomenon in our own lives, or know of people who are so sensitive to one another that they communicate without talking. It is not uncommon to detect that what a person is telling you is not the truth. Often others will tell you that they are fine, yet you know that they are not. This subtle, intuitive knowing is an example of the connection of one subjective mind to another. The subjective phase of our mind is also our contact with the Universal Mind that is God.

Objective Mind

The objective (or conscious) mind is an aspect of mind where we make choices. Do I drive to work the regular way or do I take an alternative route? Do I have cereal or eggs for breakfast? Do I earn my living as a computer programmer or as a carpenter? This is the phase of mind that has programmed the personal belief system. This is the place where we have chosen the state of our health, the condition of our finances, the circumstances in our relationships. It can also be used to change those beliefs if they no longer serve a useful purpose in your life.

The conscious mind is also the start point of creativity. This is the place where ideas are born and turned to the subjective mind for development. It is the part of mind with which we think.

I believe that we are on this earth for a purpose. That purpose is our own Spiritual Growth. The desires within us are God given, designed to move us toward that growth. The issues that seem to interfere with our happiness are exactly the lessons we need to move us along the path of spiritual evolution. The objective mind is where we make decisions to move toward that growth or away from it.

Subjective Mind

The term subjective (or subconscious) mind has been used to refer to all that dwells in thought beyond our awareness. There is no particular part of the brain that can be identified as the subconscious. It is a part of the mind (that which is thought) not the brain (that which is physical.) It is a relief to know that we do not have to think about every breath we take. We do not consciously command our heart to pump blood throughout our circulatory system. We do not direct our hands in the motions needed to direct a forkful of food into our mouth. All of this is done by our autonomic nervous system. We are not even consciously aware of the complex activities of the digestive system, which breaks down our food into the nutrients that our body needs for growth and survival.

All of the experiences we have had in our lives, all impressions, perceptions, and memory are stored in our subjective mind. Many of these we can consciously recall. Some we do et even though they are not consciously remembered, u.., main in our subjective mind.

The subconscious mind holds our beliefs about ourselves, about the people around us, the way things are and the way things work. Some of these are personal belief systems that refer to our own lives and the way we live them. Some of them came from what we call the "race consciousness." These are the memories, impressions or experiences that we have accepted without having consciously thought. These are the accepted ideas of humankind, or the culture into which we were born. These beliefs affect, control, limit, or expand our entire lives.

As an example of a race consciousness belief, we all seem to accept the idea that our "group" is somehow superior to someone else's "group". The group may refer to a political party, or a religious faith that we accept. It may be the town where we were raised, or the one we chose to live in as adults. It may be the company that employs us, the social organization we have joined, or identification with a hobby or avocation that we pursue. This belief, that our group is superior, is an unconscious idea, rarely chosen, rarely questioned. It often leads to great personal unhappiness and can isolate us from people that have valuable ideas that can improve our lives. In some cases this sense of superiority has led tragically to war or murder. An example of this is that part of the world called "Fertile Crescent" at the western end of the Mediterranean Sea, particularly, Syria, Israel, Jordan, Iran, Iraq, Saudi Arabia, and Egypt. Here Moses, Jesus, and Mohammed were born. For thousands of years the race consciousness of the people in that area has been intolerant and hateful, waging war with one another. When Jesus said, *"Love thy neighbor as thyself"* (Matthew 19:19), he did not say, "Love only those neighbors who are members of your group."

An example of a personal belief system is this: When I was a child my mother emphasized the danger of getting wet. I remember being told not to get my feet wet, or my head wet, to come in out of the rain and not to play in puddles. Sure enough, throughout my entire life I would get sick during rainy weather. Then one day I discovered the joy and adventure of moving a small boat across a body of water powered by sail alone. Sailing by its very nature is a wet activity. With more experience one will venture out in stronger winds and higher seas and get even more thoroughly and ecstatically drenched. One day I noticed that I never became ill (caught a cold) just by being wet. My belief system shifted and since then the weather has no effect on my health.

What has an effect on health is subconsciously held beliefs. When we make a conscious effort to change these beliefs, the effects around us change as well. The objective mind is the area of "programming." The subjective mind is the creative part that accepts the "program" and creates the life we experience.

Subjective mind is a far greater concept than our individual minds. We believe that it is a Universal subjectivity. Each individual mind has an atmosphere within this universal field. It is this universality into which we pray.

Physical, Mental, Spiritual

We humans live life on three levels, the physical, mental, and spiritual. Our body and all our effects: homes, cars, clothes, jobs, etc., represent the physical level. The mental is the way we think, and what we think, the choices we make today, the decisions we have made in the past. The spiritual level is that which goes beyond body and mind. It is something that we don't see or perhaps understand, but we sense, know, that there is a part of us that is our essence. It is closely connected with our belief in a Higher Power

Although it would be preferable to live in perfect balance among the three realms, we normally pay more attention to one than another. We shift from one level to another depending upon circumstances in our lives. The physical is the most obvious. Our attention is on whether we are healthy, sick, strong or weak. Do we live comfortably, make an acceptable income, and enjoy healthy relationships? Or are we just barely getting by, always worried and feeling lonely? These are manifestations of our belief system. The intellect becomes more important in many of life's situations on the job, studying, or solving problems. The creativity and inventiveness we demonstrate and the value of our decisions indicates the level of our intelligence. The spiritual realm is less obvious and sometimes gets less attention than it deserves. We are all spiritual beings, all individualized expressions of God. However, it sometimes takes a dramatic event to get our attention tuned to the spiritual part of life.

There is in humankind an evolutionary process that moves us from the physical to the intellectual to the spiritual. We can see development throughout an individual's life. The young live in the physical realm of high activity, testing themselves and others. During the productive working years people use their intelligence to accomplish more with less effort. As humans mature they gain a better understanding of the spiritual values of life.

This evolutionary process can be traced through history. Throughout most of mankind's history we lived in the physical realm. Work was accomplished by physical strength, slowly, with much effort. With every intellectual development there has been a reduction of physical labor. Now we are in the information age, when intellect reigns. We are beginning to see a shift toward the spiritual. More people are turning to spiritual, and/or religious practices. This also includes the practice or participation in eastern philosophies such as yoga, Tai Chi, forms of meditation or prayer and the proliferation of twelve step groups. An increase in church attendance is another indication of this shift.

Spiritual Mind Treatment

Spiritual Mind Treatment is a structured form of affirmative prayer. Spiritual means relating to the nature of Spirit or God. Spiritual Mind Treatment is an effective form of prayer that can be used by anyone who makes the effort to learn it.

We believe that the mind of each individual is connected to the Universal Mind of God. We acknowledge that connection in the prayer. Our mind contains within it the system of beliefs by which our lives are led. It is this belief system that we affect and change through treatment.

We use the term treatment because it is a healing structure. What is being healed is the system of beliefs within us. It clears our thoughts of that which is untrue, of doubts and fears. In treatment (affirmative prayer) we are conscious of the awareness that this prayer is answered according to our individual beliefs.

We do not deny the condition that exists. We see beyond the condition into the perfection of the circumstance or individual, as an expression of God. We affirm that perfection. What we treat is our own mind. What we pray with is our conscious mind. The atmosphere we pray into is the Universal Mind. The part that is affected is our sub-conscious mind.

During affirmative prayer we are using the objective mind as "programmer" to change the beliefs held in our subjective mind. We consciously decide what changes we want in our lives and create the prayer around those specific changes. The prayer then works upon the subjective mind to begin the creative process of altering the belief.

In this form of prayer we are dealing with the natural laws of the universe. As Luke 17:21 says, *"The Kingdom of God is within you."* We use the natural laws of mind to touch that kingdom within and change our beliefs. The change in beliefs changes the physical manifestations.

In this book you will find many prayers. These are given only as illustrations. The most effective prayer for you comes from the conviction behind your words, not mine or anyone else's.

During the learning process it is preferable that all treatments be in the written form. This gives you a chance to correct, rewrite, or edit them at any time. The very act of taking the time to write improves the clarity of the prayer. Keeping written treatments over the years is also a good way to check and appreciate your progress. Like anything else, praying improves with practice. After 15 years, I still write treatments, although most of the prayers I create for myself are silent and those for other people are spoken aloud so the person for whom I pray can hear them.

We do not pray in a supplicating manner. We are not asking favors from a judging God. Our God is a God of love. The God that created us expresses through us. As we live more fully, vitally, creatively, so God lives. Spirit is continually pouring blessings upon us. However, most of us do not receive these blessings as well as we might. Our prayer affects our increased ability to receive what God gives us.

If you are reading this book it is a fair assumption that you desire to make a change in some part of your life, that you feel something is missing or that something could be better. Do not neglect these desires. That is Spirit within you driving you toward your own higher spiritual growth. Most of these desires fall within the physical level of existence and have to do with health, abundance or relationships. The difference between what your condition is presently and what you desire has to do with one of your current beliefs. These beliefs can be changed. The method of changing them is called Spiritual Mind Treatment, or affirmative prayer. Treatment may be described as an exercise of one praying to change his or her beliefs about a condition or thing. It is the action of the objective (or conscious) mind upon the subjective (or subconscious) mind to manifest improved conditions.

The Gospel of John begins with the sentence *"In the beginning was the word, and the word was with God. The word was God and the word was made flesh."* (John 1:1,14) So our treatments begin with our word, that word (idea) is with God, and is made flesh (turned into form).

For more information on the subject of mind or the background and development of the idea of Spiritual Mind Treatment, I heartily recommend the book, "The Science of Mind" by Dr. Ernest Holmes. (See suggested readings at end of book.)

CHAPTER TWO

INTRODUCTION TO SPIRITUAL MIND TREATMENT
THE FIVE BASIC STEPS OF TREATMENT

The standard form of Spiritual Mind Treatment has five steps. In a later chapter there are examples of other forms of treatment, such as the three step, the one-step and instant treatment. For the most part, these other forms are derivatives of the standard five-step form of treatment. The title of this book is Seven Steps to Effective Prayer. The additional two steps, although they may not be written or spoken, can be important to the prayer for some people.

The five steps are:
1) Recognition
2) Unification
3) Affirmation or Realization
4) Gratitude or Acceptance
5) Release

There is an introduction to each step in this chapter. Subsequently there is an entire chapter devoted to explaining the function and purpose of each step.

Within the chapters on each step there are examples given as illustrations. The examples are to assist you in writing prayers for yourself. During the learning process I believe the five steps should be written.

Step One - Recognition

The purpose of step one is to recognize the existence of a Higher Power. To acknowledge this Power as the Source, Creator, Energy, God, Christ, or whatever name is most meaningful for you. The step could begin: "God is...". This beginning is followed by the attributes of God as you see and know God, and those attributes that apply to the particular treatment being done.

For example: if the treatment is for prosperity or abundance it is well to recognize God as the Source of all things. Whether it be the universe itself, the planet earth, the trees and flowers that grow upon it, each individual person and the products of human effort such as cars, houses, clothing, tools. God is within all of these. If all humankind and all things are expressions of God, then abundance and prosperity are expressions of God's creativity.

Step Two - Unification

As we understand that there is one God, we will understand that God is the Creator of every thing and is part of each creation. We will accept the idea that the Source is within you, me, mountains, maple trees, Mars, and mosquitoes. God is everywhere and in all things. God is the unification of all things. This is called "Oneness." Within this "Oneness" our individual mind is a part of the Mind of God. Each person on earth is an individual expression of that Higher Power. The mind that we are treating through our prayer is our own mind and it is always connected to the Divine Mind of the Universe. So the purpose of the second step is to make a conscious connection with our Higher Power.

At first glance one might say. "All right, I accept that idea, but if we are always connected to God, why should we have to write out a prayer, or spend any time thinking about it?"

We unify with our Higher Power because in the midst of our humanity, our busy-ness with job, home, family, school, hobbies, all of the activities we are inclined to pursue, we often are not conscious of our Oneness with the Higher Power. The time when we are most inclined to turn to prayer is when we are in pain or dire need. That pain may be physical, mental, or emotional. In the midst of that pain, we are most likely to forget that God exists, loves us, and is part of us, and part of the pain as well. Step Two, the Unification Step brings us to the awareness of oneness <u>consciously</u>.

The basic form of the second step is to recognize and state that whatever God is, I am. For example, if the treatment has to do with relationships, the first step may say, "God is love." The second step may also say "I am love." A treatment for health may begin, "God expresses Itself in the perfection of health and vitality." The second step may be, "I am one with God's perfect healing energy."

Step Three - Affirmation or Realization

In the third step we affirm that what we desire is ours right now. We speak in the first person with emotion, power and knowledge of success. "I know!" We speak in the present tense. "It is!" What we desire is ours right now, not coming at some indeterminate time in the future. Speak with authority, knowing that we have already identified God as being within that which we desire and the source of that which we desire. Knowing that since we are a part of that God, our word acting through God's natural laws becomes the creation of that experience in our life. This can be an emotional process. That is fine. The more thought or emphasis that is placed on this step as written or spoken, the more powerful it can be.

At its simplest form the third step may only include the words "I know" followed by whatever it is you are affirming. In most cases, the longer the step is and the more fully and completely the affirmation is worded, the clearer the treatment becomes.

Step Four - Gratitude or Acceptance

Since we pray in the present tense and in the affirmative, we believe that the treatment is effective immediately. God has already given us everything that we need for a joyous, abundant, happy, creative life. We simply need to accept and be <u>conscious</u> of these gifts that are already ours. As we would thank a friend for a gift given to us, so we also thank our Higher Power for the gift bestowed upon us as the result of this prayer. Therefore, step four often starts with phrases such as, "With gratitude," or "I accept." For example: "I accept my beautiful new car knowing that it is God's creation." However, at its simplest form, "Thank you" is sufficient. Any addition is for the purpose of clarifying our gratitude for God's grace.

Step Five - Release

Step Five, the Release step, is more than a closing. It is releasing any doubt, knowing that the treatment is complete and that the demonstration has already manifested. This step may reiterate the purpose of the treatment as defined in the first two steps. It may partially repeat the specific request as affirmed in the third step.

The closing of the prayer can be simply "Amen" which has been used for many years in closing and releasing prayer. A phrase, such as "And so it is," is often used.

Simplified or Basic Treatment

For the purpose of clarity, most of the steps consist of a few sentences. However, step three, the affirmation step may be several paragraphs. A prayer should be as long as is necessary to clarify the knowledge that the desired results are in effect within the mind of the person speaking or writing the treatment. However, a prayer can also be a very simple statement. A simplified, easy to remember basic form of treatment is:

God is.
I am.
I know... (clearly affirm the desired effect).
Thank you.
Good-bye.

This basic form is a good place to begin using Spiritual Mind Treatment. Although each of the five steps is explained more thoroughly in the following chapters, this simplified form can be used immediately.

CHAPTER THREE

THE FIRST STEP
RECOGNITION

The first step of Spiritual Mind Treatment (Affirmative Prayer) begins by recognizing and using the name that defines for us the existence of the oneness of the Higher Power.

We address the Higher Power invoking the authority of that Universal Mind. We recognize that all that is, ever was, ever will be, or can be, is from or of this creative mind power. It is the time to recognize the Higher Power as we would recognize a friend who has just stepped into the room. Do not slip quickly past this step. The more time that is taken, the more effort going into recognizing the Power that is at work, the easier the rest of the treatment flows.

In the previous chapter I state, "God is" can be an adequate beginning for our treatments. This is a good phrase to use when first learning to write a treatment. It can also suffice when one has enough experience writing treatments that the full comprehension and enormity of that simple phrase are realized.

In many cases it is preferable to find other names for God, that are more in alignment with the specific prayer being written. Let us not limit our concept of God by using only one name. Be creative and flexible. As we pray more often and create more specific prayers for others and ourselves, there is a danger of getting into an inflexible, routine format. This tends to stifle creativity and limit the power of the prayer. One of the things that renders memorized prayers ineffective is that they are spoken by rote. It is as if we hear a familiar song on the radio. We have heard it so many times before that we no longer listen.

There are also those who have a resistance to using the word "God," as it signifies to them a critical and condemning judge. Perhaps Higher Power, Nature, Energy, or Creator would suit them better. In my late teens I rejected religion and the concept of a judging God. My experience is not unlike that of many others. For many years I refused to enter anything that called itself a church or any other named religious institution. At that time I believed that religions were systems perpetrated by self-proclaimed authorities to control others through guilt and manipulation. However, I did believe there was a Higher Power. I realized through my science and engineering education that the universe was too perfectly formed to have happened by accident. There must be a guiding force of some kind directing the process. If the word God meant a judging condemning entity, I would not have that God in my life. The name I could accept as my Higher Power was "Energy."

I accept that mass is usually a quantity of material substance. The earth has mass, as does your body, an automobile, a twenty dollar bill, a cancer cell, other people in our life. Einstein's Theory of Relativity gives the formula $E=MC^2$ as its most basic premise. When mass is accelerated to a sufficient speed it turns into pure energy. Mass becomes energy; energy is converted back to mass. Energy becomes the things, the effects of life. A spiritual mind treatment converts thought energy through the belief system of your mind into the manifestations of life that surround you.

We are surrounded at all times by undifferentiated energy, which at some point of concentration becomes mass or form. Treatment directs energy to flow into the form of our choosing. We are always choosing. In many cases we are allowing our subconscious beliefs to make our choices for us. We can make a difference by choosing consciously. Conscious choice directs energy into creating the kind of life we desire for ourselves.

At its highest form, the recognition step allows us to feel the presence of God surrounding us with love and grace. With that feeling awareness of being in the presence of God we know that all gifts are already given. We open ourselves up to receive.

When I first began to do Spiritual Mind Treatment, I used "energy" as the word I would accept for God. Now it is time for you to find the words that you can accept. So take a few minutes right now, pick up a pencil and on the following page make your own list of names for the Source of the Universe. DO IT! I know it is easier to sit and read. However, if there were not an issue in your life that needed resolution, you would not be reading this book. Take the time. You will not regret it. Was Jesus speaking to you when he said, *"The Kingdom of God does not come by observation,"* Luke 17:20?

NAMES FOR GOD

Welcome back. In the first step recognition - we may want to include some of the attributes of God. What are the attributes of God? We speak of God as Omniscient, Omnipresent, and Omnipotent. Omni means all or universal. So God is all knowing, present everywhere, and unlimited in creative power.

For example, if we are treating for prosperity we might say, "The Creator of the Universe is abundant." In a treatment dealing with relationships we may begin, "Divine Energy flows through love." A treatment for a health issue may start "All Knowing Wisdom manifests in the perfection of a healthy body."

Can you think of other attributes of God? It is time once again to find that pencil and make a list that is your own creation. Do it now.

ATTRIBUTES OF GOD

That was not too hard. You can add to the list at any time. It will be a wonderful source for your own treatments.

Here are a few sample Recognition steps:

Purpose: To remove limitations.
> I celebrate the knowledge that within the creative power of the Universal Mind there is only freedom, abundance, and love. Spirit is unlimited. In the Mind of God, all is divine, all is limitless.

Purpose: To love and be loved more.
> I Acknowledge the Divine Loving Source of the Universe. Within Divine Order, all is love. All creation is made manifest for the expression of love at all times, in all ways.

Purpose: Greater receptivity to abundance.
> I understand that all manifestations are the result of the action of Spiritual Source on mind. That within the nature of this Power all things are possible, all desires met, all demonstrations already exist.

Purpose: Divine right action in all events.
> I recognize at this moment the omnipresent existence of the One Mind. All intelligence, all knowledge, all abundance, exists within the Creator of the Universe. In God there is only Divine right action, growth, well being and unconditional, unlimited Love.

Use this space to write your own Recognition Steps

CHAPTER FOUR

THE SECOND STEP
UNIFICATION

During the second step of prayer, we consciously and intentionally connect ourselves to that Universal Source that we described in the first step. It can be a simple statement, such as, "I am one with God." Or *"My Father art with me and I am with thee."* (John 17:21).

It is important to realize that what we change in giving a Spiritual Mind Treatment is our own mind. Our belief systems are those ideas that are related to our experiences or frame of reference and which we accept as truth. They are normally hidden from our conscious thinking. We see the effects of these beliefs as the results that manifest in our lives. To become conscious of what we believe, we need only look at our lives. Are we poor, sick, alone, or are we abundant, healthy, and surrounded by loving relationships? The lives we live are a result of those deep-rooted beliefs in our subconscious mind. The Unlimited Mind of God can change the beliefs hidden within the subconscious mind when we bring them consciously into focus.

Although the grace of Divine Love is showered upon us at all times, we are not always in a receptive mode. Our beliefs and the system of beliefs that surround us seem to say that we are not quite all right, not quite good enough. In truth, each of us is Divinely Unique. Our very existence on this planet is a miracle. There has never been nor will there ever be another person (expression of God) exactly like us.

From my personal experience, I know that I am not at the point of enlightenment where I always feel aware of my connection to my Spiritual Source. During the Unification Step we become aware that we are at one with all there is, all Spirit, all that defines the Higher Power. We get beyond the limiting ego of the personality and allow the expression of Spirit to flow through our words.

There was a time when I could be called at my place of employment by anyone who felt an urgent desire for prayer. I could be interrupted in the midst of concentrating on my job, by a person dealing with a crisis serious enough for them to pick up the telephone and ask for help. It was a wonderful learning opportunity. I had to shift my attention from the task before me to the challenge that this individual was confronting. I had to focus my mind on the pain expressed, ask appropriate questions to determine the exact purpose of the treatment, then to pray, hang up the phone and return to business. The Unification Step became very important to me during those times. I learned to make it as long as necessary to focus on my connection to the Higher Power and trust that Spirit will flow through my words.

To begin step two, it is essential to consider our relationship with our personal Higher Power. If God is omnipresent, present in all things at all times, then God is always present in you and in me. The beginning of the second step is for me to affirm that presence. I say, "God is." "I am." "My mind is part of the Universal Mind."

The next part of the Unification Step is to state our connection with the attributes of God. Refer to your list in Chapter Three for Step One, the Recognition step. There is nothing wrong with repeating, word for word, the list that you have previously prepared; however, it does lack interest and creativity. As you become more focused on your Higher Power, you become more aware of the attributes and find it easier to verbalize them.

As each person is unique, the manner in which we connect to Spirit is unique. Take the time to find your own individual way to make that great connection. Some people are very visual and can close their eyes and picture themselves as being a single part of a great whole. For example: as a grain of sand on a long endless beach, a drop of water in a vast ocean, or a single flower in an immense garden.

Other people are more kinesthetic or tactile. They will find it helpful to use physical movement as a method of connection, such as Ti Chi, yoga, or dance. In many Native American and primitive African cultures, dancing was considered the way to be present with Spirit. People who are more kinesthetic may find it helpful to hold in their hands a soft fabric, a smooth stone, a crystal, a flower, or a meaningful medallion to assist in the process. They may feel more connected to Spirit when walking barefoot on sand or grass or by touching the bark or leaves of a tree.

Some people are more auditory and may find that soft music, chanting, repeating a sound like the expression, "OM," or using a mantra like "God is love, I am love," are ways they focus on their unification with the Universe. They often find that inspirational or classical music is the key to their awareness of unification.

Many are able to connect through a simple word that they can relate to. Thinking of God as love may be the way to feel your heart open up. Imagining your mind as a part of the All Knowing Mind, which holds all knowledge, can make you aware of your connection with the Source. The word "energy" may help you to feel the energy of the universe flowing through your body.

Take the time to discover the method that works best for you. The importance of this step is such that we are not ready to move on to the third step until we make that connection with Spirit. *"Seek ye first the kingdom of God...and all these things shall be added unto you."*

Remember, there is One Spirit, One Mind. The path you take does not matter. All paths lead to God. Try many paths, find the one most comfortable. Then, when you get really comfortable with it, try another way.

Examples of Unification Steps:

Right now and forever, I am connected with the Creator of All. My mind and the creative Mind of Spirit are one mind. I speak my word into the Law and the effects around me change.

I accept the knowledge that I am a part of Divine Consciousness. I know that my purpose is part of Universal Purpose. My life is an important part of creation.

My energy is a part of the Energy of the Universe. My Creativity is part of and connected to the Creative Spirit from which all things have evolved.

I am one with the peace, comfort and safety of Universal Love. My mind, body, and spirit are one with the mind, and love of God.

USE THIS SPACE TO WRITE YOUR OWN UNIFICATION STEPS

CHAPTER FIVE

THE THIRD STEP
AFFIRMATION OR REALIZATION

"So God created man in his own image; male and female he created them. And God blessed them and God said to them, be fruitful, and multiply, and fill the earth." Genesis 1:27-28.

We are God's means to be, the way God expresses upon this earth. We are in this world to sow our seeds (thoughts) and reap the harvest (demonstrations). We are not here to limit ourselves, to live in suffering, sickness, poverty, and loneliness. Our desires are God's gifts, the images of what our lives may become. They are to be expressed not suppressed. The more abundantly each of us expresses life, the greater he or she demonstrates God's glory.

Do not be afraid to desire a better life for yourself. That is God's desire speaking within you, demanding to be expressed. There is no need to feel guilt or undeserving of affirming and claiming what you want. *"Ask, and it will be given you; seek, and you will find; knock, and it will be opened unto you. For every one who asks receives, and he who seeks finds, and to him who knocks it will be opened."* Matthew 7:7-8 and Luke 11:9-10). We are instructed to seek improvement and growth in every area of our life. Who are we to limit ourselves by not accepting the gifts Spirit abundantly gives?

A Spiritual Mind Treatment is not a prayer of supplication. We are not begging. We are not asking God for anything.

God already gives us everything. The issue lies not in God's giving but in our receiving. Because of our belief system, which conditions our subconscious mind, we may not readily accept the gifts God provides. Through prayer, we can change our belief to be aware of and accepting more of Gods bounty. *"It is your Fathers good pleasure to give you the Kingdom."* (Luke 12:32.)

We are immersed in and surrounded by the living substance of Infinite Power, All Potential, and Unlimited Abundance. It comes into our experience as we live It, be It, act as though It is so. The realization step is the heart of the treatment. Up until now we have simply acknowledged that there is a Higher Power in the universe and that we are treating our own mind to accept the good that is showered upon us. Now we state powerfully, positively, that we are God's expression of Life.

The Realization step is to be written as a powerful, affirmative, current statement, knowing that what we are praying for has already been given. There are a few guidelines that make this step easier and more effective. First, it is best to state the desired result in a simple straight forward manner. Be as specific as possible. Write your statement in an affirmative manner. Write it in the present tense. Do not tell God how to provide the result; simply state that what is desired has been realized. Finally, do not limit God's grace by using limiting words in your affirmation.

What is the expected result of a treatment? It is a healing or a demonstration of what is desired, a change in the belief and therefore in the life of the person for whom the prayer was designed. We need to state this result in the treatment clearly and directly. Flowery words and creative poetic writing are not necessary. We simply state that we already have the desired result. God has already provided for us. All we need to do is be open and receptive. We need to remind ourselves, to convince ourselves. This is why we say, "I know, I have, or I am."

Make the treatment as specific as possible. An example would be: A man needs transportation for his job and is required to carry machinery and equipment and tow a trailer. Do not describe the vehicle but what the need is, as your Higher Power could provide something far greater than what you have in mind. A treatment for basic transportation may mean a bicycle. A treatment for a health issue requires that we describe the desired result. This may be perfect health, complete cure, energy, vitality, and ability to live life fully.

It is equally important to be sure the treatment is stated in a positive, rather than a negative manner. Affirm what you do want, rather than what you don't want. Instead of writing "There is no more cancer," say "All cells in the body are glowing with radiant health." Instead of "I am not broke," say, "I accept Spirit's unlimited abundance." Instead of "I am not alone," write, "I live in a world of harmonious, satisfying relationships."

All treatments are to be in the present tense. Within the Omnipresence that is God there is no past and future. There is only now, this very moment. One of the most common mistakes made by those beginning to learn treatment is to slip into the future tense. Tense is a contrivance and limitation of human thought. Examples: Abundance is coming soon, instead of abundance is mine right now. I will be promoted; instead of I am now performing my wonderful new job.

We do not have to tell God <u>how</u> to bring about the result. The Omniscient God has already provided for us. If we want a perfect place to live, it is not necessary to pick out a particular house that we like and pray for it. The people who live there now may be quite content to stay without our interference. The perfect home for us already exists and is waiting for us to notice it. If we want a romantic relationship it is best not to pray to capture someone else's spouse. The perfect companion, friend, lover and teacher is waiting for us. The prayer opens the channel for us to accept God's guidance.

Sometimes, by our attempts to tell God how to assist us, we limit ourselves. Desiring more abundance, we may pray for a $100 a week raise, whereby treating for unlimited prosperity we get much more. By understanding that our prosperity comes from God, not our employer, we will realize that income can flow to us in many ways. Wanting a relationship, we may pray for someone with physical beauty and get incompatibility. Whereby treating for a perfect life companion, we receive the love we desire in our life. Wishing a healing, we might pray to relieve the symptoms, rather than for the cause to be revealed and trusting the healing that is taking place.

It is wise to remember that all that appears as negative effects in our lives are the symptoms of an underlying cause. They are the results of belief systems and subsequent behavior, actions or inactions that has led to this situation or condition. It is important to understand the root of the problem, the underlying belief. For example: a man has a headache and wishes to feel better and prays that the head is pain free. However, if he knows the cause of the headache is tension between himself and a coworker, a treatment should be done for a harmonious working relationship. In this circumstance, as the relationship improves the headache disappears. Chapter nine gives more information about defining the purpose of an individual prayer.

Examples of Realizations Steps:

For clarity of purpose:

> My purpose in life is now revealed clearly to me. All of my experiences have led to the knowledge and use of this Divine Purpose. All of my likes and dislikes, all of the gifts that were provided for the fulfillment of my life, are part of this purpose. All that I have learned has come to be used for the benefit of God, the world, and myself, as a part of this purpose. I move forward confi-

dently into each day knowing that more is revealed with every step. That which was unclear yesterday is obvious today. As I accept God's love and proceed with each day's task, I know that I am fulfilling my purpose and being fulfilled by it.

For a consciousness of prosperity:

I know that at this moment the abundance of Spirit surrounds me. My consciousness sees only the good, only the richness that is bestowed upon me. My mental attitude is one of abundance at all times. All good flows through me. Money comes to me easily from a wide variety of sources. My thoughts and actions reflect prosperity.

For being a conduit for Spirit:

The Energy of the Universe flows through me at all times in this day so that energy flows out to the spirit of each one that I contact. With every interaction I have we both benefit. Every one I touch feels surrounded by the love and grace of spirit.

USE THIS SPACE TO WRITE YOUR OWN
AFFIRMATION STEPS

CHAPTER SIX

THE FOURTH STEP
GRATITUDE AND ACCEPTANCE

The Source of the Universe contains and provides everything that we need or desire. We receive as much "good" as we are able or willing to accept. *"For it is the Father's good pleasure to give you the kingdom,"* (Luke 12:32). Consider how much we have been given: from the miracle of life itself, to our current state of health, knowledge, wisdom and education. Most of us live in homes with indoor plumbing, electricity, and adequate heat. We own automobiles, TV's, furniture, clothes, tools and appliances. We live far beyond the standard of Jesus and his disciples, far beyond our ancestors of even one hundred years ago. A short inventory of our possessions and the consideration of what life would be like without them should fill even the poorest with gratitude.

Yet, it is natural that we all want more. We want to improve the quality of what we have, such as trading in the Chevrolet for a Cadillac or selling the three-bedroom ranch house and moving to a four bedroom colonial. We yearn for the things we do not have such as the sports car to get to the supermarket faster, or the four wheel drive range buster to go where there are no supermarkets. One of the principles taught in Economics 101 is that human needs are never totally satisfied. I call this God's Divine Discontent. Since God provides everything and is unlimited in giving, what we receive is what we believe that we deserve. It is what we <u>accept</u> for ourselves.

So in the fourth step of treatment we declare our acceptance of that which we affirmed in the third step. As one would thank a friend for a gift, we thank the Higher Power for providing the demonstration of our prayer. *"Oh Father, I thank thee for though hast heard me."* (John 11:41).

Sometimes we find that our ability to receive and accept God's gifts is limited. If this is the case there is more work that we must do inside ourselves to allow us to accept the good that is bestowed upon us. The cause can be a low level self-esteem that does not believe that we are deserving of having that which we desire.

At one time I wanted my own sailboat. I treated for it and found a unique vessel at a ridiculously low price. I also found a slip available in a marina close to my home that previously had a five-year waiting list. I almost did not take it. Although I wanted a boat, my self-esteem was such that a part of me felt that I was unworthy of one. I wrote a treatment to know that I was worthy of and accepting of this beautiful sailboat. When I finally moved forward and bought the boat, I named it "Acceptance" and painted the name on it in large letters. It became a constant reminder that God's gifts are freely given, and we need only have to raise our belief to know that God loves us and provides what we desire. We need only to be open, receptive, accepting and grateful to our Higher Power.

Therein is the purpose of this step. The Universe provides abundantly for our needs. We have to learn how to receive. I found it a valuable exercise to write the treatment to increase my ability to accept God's gifts. Some may find it valuable to take an inventory, notice all the things that have already been accepted, and the gratitude that surrounds them.

Step Four is a simple step, one or two sentences or as long as necessary, to acknowledge that we do accept and are grateful for the demonstration.

Examples of Gratitude and Acceptance:

With gratitude, I accept this abundance as my divine inheritance as a child of the Universal Spirit.

Thank you Higher Power for the love shown to me. For the love that I receive and the love that I give.

Gratitude and joy fill my soul with the relationship of each person I know. I am so happy to connect with each friend in my life.

Thank you Divine Creator for guiding me to this perfect place. For creating it to support my growth in every way, and for the peace that exists here.

USE THIS SPACE TO WRITE YOUR OWN GRATITUDE STEPS

CHAPTER SEVEN

THE FIFTH STEP
RELEASE

Although a short, often one sentence step, the importance of the Release Step cannot be overlooked. This is the time when we let go and allow God to work.

There have been books written about our need to release the past in order to move into the future. This can be letting go of our parents to step into adulthood, letting go of a job that is not satisfying so that we can move on to a better one. It can also be letting go of the clothes that are old and worn or no longer fit us, so there is room in the closet for new clothes. Letting go of that which no longer meets our needs or provides for our growth is vital in allowing the process of moving on to begin. So it is necessary to let go of the treatment, to release it knowing that it is complete, and the message delivered. It is time to allow Spirit to work.

This does not mean that we can never say another prayer for the same purpose. We continue to do treatment until the desired result is manifested in our lives. We may create a new one tomorrow, or next week. Tomorrow's prayer is a new prayer and will have its own life. Worrying over the old, rerunning it in our mind, probing, criticizing, and harassing it does not help.

We also need to understand that we do not "make" things happen. We speak our word in prayer and release it. Universal Mind does the work. *"The words that I speak, I do not speak of myself; but my Father who abides with me does these works."* (John 14:10)

My favorite closing to a prayer is simply "Amen." Amen means, "sealed in trust, faith, and truth." Many people use the phrase, "And so it is!" Meaning that the prayer is completed and turned over to the working of natural law, knowing and accepting that the payer is fulfilled. *"Behold, I make all things new."* (Rev. 21:5)

Examples of Release Steps:

> Knowing that God always responds and that this treatment is complete, I release it into Universal Mind. Amen

> I speak this treatment into the Law, the Soul of the Universe, the Spirit that changes the effects of my life, knowing that it is complete. And so it is.

> This treatment is released into the Law of Mind, which even now is doing the work. Amen

> I release this treatment into Universal Law, the part of Divine Energy that does not question but that changes my words into the effects of my life. And so it is.

USE THIS SPACE TO WRITE YOUR OWN RELEASE STEPS

CHAPTER EIGHT

OTHER FORMS OF TREATMENT

Although the standard form of treatment is done in five clearly separate steps, there are other forms of treatment. In some cases these are simply combinations of the five steps. During the process of learning the structure and form of treatment, I suggest that you write each step as a separate paragraph.

Three Step Treatment: In most cases a three-step treatment incorporates all five steps. Usually the first two steps are merged. Combining the Recognition and Unification steps as when Jesus said, *"The Father and I are one."* The Fourth and Fifth step can also be combined. Gratitude and Release steps can be stated as "With a grateful heart, I release this treatment to my Higher Power.

Creative Thought Magazine, a monthly publication (see Suggested Reading in appendix), features a treatment for each day. These are excellent, professionally-written treatments, and they can be used to effect great changes in an individual's life. They are also excellent learning tools. They are written in the three-step format. However, with careful analysis you will notice the five steps and the gracious way in which they are combined. If you call or write to Creative Thought they will tell you where an issue can be purchased.

One Step Treatment: A one step treatment usually means an affirmation. It can be powerful, useful, and easy to remember and is often repeated over and over each day. Although affirmations can have great value, they are not complete treatments. I believe that they are a good supplement to other forms of treatment. However, for me, I feel something is missing. I believe that each step: 1 and 2, Recognition and Unification, then 3, Affirmation, followed by 4 and 5, Gratitude and Release, is important. There is more on affirmations in Chapter Ten.

Science of Mind Magazine (see suggested readings) publishes one-step treatments (affirmations) as part of their Daily Guides to Richer Living. This is an inspirational reading for each day. This magazine also contains other articles of an expansive and inspirational nature. It is sold in Religious Science churches, B. Dalton and other bookstores, and many large newsstands. If you call or write to them they will send an information package.

Instant Treatments: in our 65-mile per hour, microwave able, on-line society; it is probably not surprising that the concept of instant prayer exists. Although my preference is to take whatever time is needed for my prayer there are occasions when immediate comfort is sought. This is a good place for a one step treatment or affirmation.

For example: suppose you are driving along a highway and see an accident. Unless trained in first aid, there is probably nothing you can actively do for those involved other than call 911 on a cellular phone if available. However, a prayer seems appropriate for OUR OWN peace of mind. Please notice that I am talking about praying for ourselves, not those involved in the accident. Praying for others is discussed thoroughly in another chapter.

Examples of instant treatments for this situation may be:

I know that God is here and all is well.

Divine Right Action is happening right now.

My safety is assured through my Higher Power. Universal Energy is working everywhere at all times. The Love of Creative Grace surrounds us.

God is. I am. Peace. Thank you. Amen.

Visualization treatment: This a treatment without words. Since I am more auditory than visual it is a challenge for me. Some people who tend to be more visually perceptive may find it easier.

Go through the same five steps by visualizing them instead of saying them or writing them. Do not add words. In the first step, picture your own image for God. In the second step, imagine how you are appearing united with God. In the third, personify the effect you desire to achieve. See it, feel it, smell it, touch it, taste it. Surround yourself with the embodiment of your new life. In the fourth step, feel gratitude and in the fifth, sense release.

I do not recommend this in the beginning stages of learning treatment. It is best at that time to write the prayers out, clearly identifying each step. However, once the steps come easily, the prayer without words is a powerful exercise.

CHAPTER NINE

THE STEP BEFORE THE STEPS
THE PURPOSE OF THE PRAYER

During the exercise of learning the individual steps of Spiritual Mind Treatment, we have assumed that the purpose of the prayer was clearly understood. The five basic steps of Spiritual Mind Treatment are what I call the framework or the skeleton of the prayer. They are the structure upon which the individual prayer is built and developed. Before we begin to write a prayer the purpose should be clearly defined. When sudden traumatic situations occur in or lives, it can be easy to determine the purpose of our treatment. However, sometimes we are dealing with changes in life-long situations with which we have become dissatisfied. Then it can be difficult to determine with clarity the purpose of our prayer. This is because the underlying cause of the dissatisfaction is not obvious. We need to search out the original condition, the underlying belief that needs to be addressed.

It is my habit to pray both morning and evening. The purpose of the morning prayer is to affirm a successful day. I know that any task that needs to be accomplished is done to the best of my ability. I know that I will have a safe trip if I am traveling. I know that if a meeting is on the agenda, it results in the highest and best good for all involved. My prayer is a reminder that I will be a beneficial presence in the lives of all that I meet, and to remember that I am connected to Spirit at all times. My evening prayer is one of thanksgiving for the day and a peaceful night's sleep. At first daily prayer seemed like a good way to practice and learn treatment. Now it is a valuable part of my routine. It is a constant reminder that I am a spiritual being having a human experience, yet always connected to Spirit.

There are times in our lives when we experience trauma, or disaster. Times when prayer is needed and the purpose makes itself readily apparent. These can be periods of intense spiritual growth. The times when we enter our "40 days in the wilderness." In the Bible the number forty is used to indicate an indefinite period of time.

Traumatic incidents usually begin with a voice. It may be the bosses' voice saying, "You are fired!" It may be the wife's voice saying, "Good-bye forever!" A voice on the phone that says, "This is the garage calling about your car." A voice may say, "This is the police, are you the mother of...?" Usually following this voice is our own voice saying, "Oh God!" Spirit has led you into the first step of treatment. Continue the steps.

In many cases the purpose of the prayer is not as clearly presented. This lack of clear purpose often leads to disappointment and discouragement; the feeling that prayer does not work or is not answered. At those times we often pray for relief of symptoms rather than correction of the cause of the circumstance. The real issue that has created the current situation is often a belief that is hidden far beneath the surface. It may be difficult to find, understand, and deal with. Professional help may be required to assist in determining the deep-seated beliefs that are creating these effects.

An example could be: a deep-rooted belief that anybody who has vast wealth is evil and has obtained it illegally. This belief can lead to a lifetime of financial problems. Have you ever heard anyone (including yourself) say, "we're poor, but honest," or, "the rich get richer and the poor get poorer." Our clichés often verbalize very deep beliefs which affect our conscious and unconscious choices.

I find it beneficial to take the time to clearly establish the issue and the desired result before I begin to pray. Sometimes I take a walk. Other times I will go into a period of meditation. One technique that helps me to define the clarity of my purpose is to have a written conversation with the issue. I sit down with a yellow pad and pencil and start with a question: "Money, where did you go?" "Body, what is wrong with you this time?" "Why am I alone?" "Now what?" "How did I get into this mess?"

This method works well because we each have our own answers deep within us. For one reason or another, we often block or deny the reality that is going on at the center of our being. I look upon this process as a dialogue between my objective or conscious mind asking the questions and my subjective or subconscious mind responding. I find it useful to print out the questions and write the answers in longhand. The answers may come rapidly. Once started, the process fills a page or two quickly. As I read my responses I gain an understanding of the issue or belief that I need to consider before starting my treatment.

We may be dealing with a deeply rooted belief. It could be an idea that was planted long ago in our subjective mind. That idea may no longer be serving us. We all know people who are never sick and others who are chronically ill. I believe either case is a manifestation of what they believe about illness. The one who is always sick may have found as a child that it was a way to get attention. At that time ill health served his desires. But at this current stage in his life, it interferes with his job, family and ambitions. It is time for this person to look at his beliefs about illness. The one who is never sick has not accepted a belief that supports illness. When we recognize and confront the belief that no longer serves us we can change it.

Before we begin writing or speaking a treatment, it is vital that we understand the issues and beliefs that we are working with and the expected result of the treatment. Since most people are able to explain the situation they are experiencing, this is the starting place in finding the underlying issue. The prayer may go more smoothly if we can state the purpose in a short sentence.

The following pages give examples of prayer treatments that deal with issues of health, abundance and relationships. Health issues usually have a hidden cause, an underlying mental equivalent that is the real reason for the condition. This mental equivalent is the belief that has created the condition. Before the prayer treatment begins, it is important to find this cause or belief.

Health

Let us say, for example, that one has caught a cold and wants to pray to eliminate the coughing, runny nose, and other symptoms. Treating the symptoms does not cure the belief that attracted the cold in the first place. Some will say that the cold was caught from coworkers, family members or others who have spread cold germs. Our bodies basically already contain all of the germs that have the potential to generate colds, flu, or pneumonia. Our immune system is designed to keep us in good health. If we catch a cold that our coworkers are enduring it is because there is something in our belief system that allows it.

The body is a reflection of our mental state. Headaches can be caused by mental confusion and worry. Vision problems can occur because there is something going on in our life that we do not want to see. Sore throat and laryngitis may indicate a repressed self expression. Heart attacks can indicate a "broken heart." A mental equivalent that allows a cold to blossom could be that we have become too busy, excessively involved in too many of life's wonderful choices, and are in a state of confusion and chaos. The brain is telling the body to slow down. Medicating ourselves with cold pills simply relieves the symptoms. This is the time to pray for clarity of God's will for us and for perfect health.

The topic of mental equivalents for disease is beyond the scope of this book. I heartily recommend Louise Hays book, *"You Can Heal Your Life."* (See recommended readings at the end of the book.) She provides a very comprehensive list of the mental equivalents for a wide variety of diseases.

The body knows how to heal itself, and can function for many years filled with vital, vibrant energy. It asks that we feed it properly, exercise it, and not poison it. However, low self-esteem and the negative beliefs hidden in the cave of our sub-conscious mind may tell us we do not deserve a long healthy life. A voice in our head may say, "Go ahead and smoke, drown your problems in alcohol, eat potato chips and donuts instead of healthy food, sit behind a desk eight hours a day and in front of the TV the rest of the night." However, through prayer we can change that voice to serve us in a fuller, more enthusiastic life.

Example of a five-step prayer treatment for perfect health:

I recognize that the Source of the Universe is perfect health and acknowledge the presence of Healing Energy right here and right now.

I celebrate my connection with the Source of all, knowing that my body is an earthly expression of the body of God. Within that body is perfect health, vitality, and strength.

I know that the healing power of Divine Mind is at work in me right now. Within my body is God's design for perfect health. The bright pure light of health is shining through me at all times. Whether awake or asleep, this power to heal is working within me every moment. I visualize my body as perfect, complete and whole, vibrant with health.

I accept my vitality and aliveness at this moment. I am grateful for the knowledge that healing energy provides me with perfect health.

I release this treatment into Universal Mind, knowing the Spirit within me is whole, perfect and complete. Amen.

Abundance

Financial problems, lack of abundance, inadequate income and unsatisfying employment, are the result of a belief that the individual does not deserve prosperity. He does not feel good enough about himself to allow God's bounty to flow into his life. In early spring I go for long walks and observe the abundance of Natures gifts. Each afternoon there are more buds on the trees and shrubs, more flowers in bloom, more birds and squirrels playing from tree to tree. The unlimited supply of God's abundance is obvious. Yet, many people live their whole lives in lack. Never having enough to quite pay all the bills. Never having savings, money for emergencies, vacations, or the extra luxuries that we all want. Many others are unhappy in their jobs, feeling unappreciated, not using their God-given talents.

As is true with health issues, there are a series of underlying beliefs that affect our prosperity. It is not in the nature of this book to employ a great deal of space to illustrate all possible issues. I will just mention some possibilities as a starting point for your own thought process.

There are legions of stories about people who have been wiped out financially through business failure, natural disaster, or some other cause, who have started over in another career and earned more money than before. We also see daily evidence of homeless people who are literally begging on the streets. The difference between the two is a belief. The one believes that the Spirit within him provides abundantly for his every need and that the failure was a learning experience from which to grow. The other believes that he got what he deserved and he belongs on the street.

The gambling casinos of Las Vegas love their high rollers. They love gamblers so much that they will pay first class airfare, provide free lodging in dreamlike accommodations, and supply them with food, drink and other expensive benefits. Who are these gamblers? Most of them are financially successful. Many have an inner belief that they do not deserve their success. They gamble as a way to punish themselves. A way to throw away the money they have received but cannot accept.

I know a man who is an attorney because his father thought he ought to be an attorney. He has had moderate success and provides well for his family. Money does not seem to be his issue. However, he has never been happy in his job. He has never had the joy and satisfaction of accomplishment. He never felt that he was contributing anything of value to the world. The statisticians of the news media tell us that most Americans are in a similar position. Whether the poor vocational choice is influenced by parents wishes, poor career counseling, advice from a hero, a peer, or whatever, many are not in satisfying, fulfilling careers. Many change careers, some successfully, some not. Others have several careers over a period of time, never quite finding their niche. Underlying the original

choice, the change, or several career changes, and the ultimate
success or failure both in terms of money and happiness, is a
belief about the individual's self worth and place in life.
A belief in poverty and lack may come from the race
consciousness of the individual's early environment. He/she
may have been born in a poor neighborhood. It may come from
his parent's belief in their own impoverished situation. It may
come from peers. We all know people with perfectly good, well
paying jobs who are always complaining about them. Whatever
the original cause, the fact is that at this time, somehow the individual believes that he/she does not deserve the abundance,
the supply, and the good that he or she desires.

The concept of Spiritual Mind Treatment is that we pray
to change our own subjective mind, our own belief. We pray
for the acceptance of God's grace. We pray for the belief that
we have all been placed on this earth for a purpose. We have
been given talents and abilities to fulfill that purpose. Those
talents are sufficient to support us well. We are all expressions
of God walking on this planet. God is not poor. God is not impoverished. We have been given all that is necessary to be productive, vital, and happy in whatever employment is best suited
to us. Along with that comes the prosperity we desire.

Example of a treatment for greater acceptance of abundance:

> I celebrate and understand that the Source of the Uni-
> verse freely and abundantly gives of Itself. That within
> the nature of God all things are possible, all desires met,
> all demonstrations already exist.

> I acknowledge that I am an expression of God's love
> placed on this earth to learn, to grow, and to demonstrate
> abundantly.

I know that right now my receptivity to abundance is enhanced fully and completely. That all thought of conditions other than complete financial freedom are released, and no longer enter my consciousness. I am conscious only of the unlimited abundance of the Universe, of the many gifts that have been provided to me. Everywhere I look, I see examples of God's abundance. I am surrounded by the freely given grace of Divine Spirit. Abundance and prosperity flow to me daily from a wide variety of sources. I speak and the Law responds with the demonstration of financial independence and financial freedom.

With gratitude, I accept this abundance as my divine inheritance as an expression of the Universal Spirit.

I release this treatment into the Law, knowing that wealth and financial security are mine.

Relationships

Relationship challenges may begin with a belief that we do not deserve to be loved. As with health and finance, there are many underlying beliefs that accumulate to influence our lives as we relate to other people. This is not a book on relationships; however, the following information may provide a place to begin discovering those issues that we need to work on using a Spiritual Mind Treatment.

We each have many types of relationships to deal with in a day or in a lifetime. Each interaction is an opportunity to grow, to learn, to express the God within us. Each of us has an opportunity to have a beneficial or a harmful effect on another human. Nowhere do we see the law of cause and effect at work as clearly as in relationships. One who gives love, joy and comfort, receives the same blessings. Another who is mean, rude and harsh in his dealings with others lives a lonely, unhappy life.

Challenges occur in all forms of relationships. However, there are significant differences in the types and seriousness of the challenges that depend upon the category of the relationship. Here are some major categories.

Primary relationship: Your relationship with yourself and with God. Note - this is the same relationship.

Secondary relationships: The close and intimate relationship with a significant other person.

Tertiary relationships: Family, parents, children, siblings, pets.

Chosen relationships: Friends that you have selected to be a part of your life.

Casual relationships: That vast body of other people who continually flow through and influence your life.

I believe that we are Spiritual Beings living a human experience. That the mind within each one of us is always connected to the Universal Mind that is the Creator of all. I believe that each one of us is an expression of that Creator on this earth. That God and each one of us are inseparable before through and after life. Our relationship with God and our relationship with our self is the same relationship.

Like all relationships there are times when it evolves beautifully, when I feel loved, cared for, and nourished. There are other times when I feel separated, abandoned, unwanted. These are times of anger and loud shouting. I am the one shouting. God listens patiently. The times of connection are the times when I love myself. The times of separation are times when that love is missing. This is the human experience! We are on this earth with spiritual lessons to be learned. We learn through our interaction with other humans.

When we are not happy with ourselves, we notice it by the way others seem to respond to us. When we feel good about ourselves, everyone else is remarkably loving.

The most significant other person in our life, or lack of such a person, is a reflection of what we believe that we deserve. We all know of people who choose another, or a succession of others to fill an emptiness, a void. Something that is missing or incomplete within themselves. When the relationship ends the other person is blamed for not having enough of whatever was needed. I am not implying that we need to be perfect ourselves before we enter another relationship. We should remember that we are all having this human experience in our own way. Remember that we are here to learn our own lessons and we choose those we share our lives with to assist us in those lessons.

I believe that in some way we choose our parents before we are born. That they are in our lives to set our paths, to establish the parameters of our experience and generate the issues that we will face that enable us to learn our life's lessons. Our job is not only to accept them and forgive them, but also to love them knowing that we chose them to direct our learning. This also applies to our siblings.

I believe that we were chosen to set our children on their paths. We do not own them. It is not our task to control every decision of their life. Our job is to love, to nourish, to teach, and to let go. Every animal in nature's kingdom has a time when the young are pushed out of the nest and made to fly on their own. Humankind has somehow missed this ritual. We tend to hold on to our children, wanting to protect them.

From the book "The Prophet" by Kahlil Gibran:

> *"Your children are not your children.*
> *They are the sons and daughters of Life's longing for it-*
> *self.*
> *They come through you but not from you.*
> *You may give them your love but not your thoughts. For*
> *they have their own thoughts.*
> *You may house their bodies but not their souls, for their*
> *souls dwell in the house of tomorrow, which you cannot*
> *visit, not even in your dreams.*
> *You may strive to be like them, but seek not to make*
> *them like you.*
> *For life goes not backward nor tarries with yesterday."*

As we choose our friends, we are choosing our teachers. As they love us, support us, betray us, or abandon us, they are fulfilling their function. Whatever issue comes up with a friend we need look no farther than our relationship with ourselves to find that same issue. Love them, for we are their teachers also.

What I have called "casual relationships" are also teachers. This includes the man who cuts you off on the highway, and the man who stops to let you through a busy intersection. The woman who jumps into the supermarket line ahead of you; and the woman who holds your baby so that you can load groceries into your car. This includes the vast array of acquaintances, coworkers, and neighbors that surround us. They are other spiritual beings having their own human experience.

A good friend once said, "I will allow anyone his own path in life. However, I do not have to follow him down it."

There was a time in my life when I used to drive aggressively. At that time the other drivers surrounding me were also aggressive. I found myself being cut off, forced from one lane to another, having to jam on my brakes to avoid a car, speed up to get out of the way of another. As I grew to find peace within myself, I noticed that the drivers around me were more peaceful. Today, I rarely meet an aggressive driver. Did <u>they</u> all change?

When I write a treatment for another person I remember that they are expressing God in the best way that they can at the time, no matter what my judgment may be. If I am affected by the actions of another, it is my mind and my belief that needs resolution. Whether the other person is the one I hold most dear in my life, or a stranger. If I am offended, upset, disoriented, angered, that is my upset and my anger.

Example of a treatment for loving relationships:

> There is a Power in the Universe that is greater than any other and I can use it for my higher good. This Power is Love, Spirit, the Creator of all. This Power exists in all relationships.
>
> I celebrate my connection with this Power of Love. Knowing that love courses through me.
>
> Love flows through me in every contact with another human being. I experience joy each time I interact with any of my friends. Every conversation is an uplifting event. I am a beneficial presence in the lives of those I meet and their presence benefits me. There is a sense of wholeness in each close relationship that I have. There is a sense of completion, a feeling that the other person is a part of my being, another segment of my soul. I learn what I can from each individual. I feel the pain and joy that they are feeling. I am connected with each.

Gratitude and joy fill my soul with the relationship of each person I know. I am so happy to be here on this earth and to know each friend.

This treatment is complete and released into the Universal Law. And so it is.

USE THIS SPACE TO WRITE A TREATMENT FOR YOURSELF

CHAPTER TEN

THE STEP AFTER THE STEPS
TAKING ACTION

The form of prayer that we call Spiritual Mind Treatment changes the effects (results) in our life by changing the beliefs that produce those effects. Once the result has been specified, and the underlying cause, belief, or mental equivalent has been identified, the treatment can be done. Once it has been written or spoken it is complete. There is no need to memorize, revise, or unnecessarily dwell on the prayer.

It is important not to agonize over a completed treatment. When a farmer plants a seed, he does not pull up the plant to see how it is growing. We must trust Nature to do the job and nourish the seed we have planted. However, as the farmer irrigates the soil and removes any weeds that grow around the plants, there may also be some additional action that we need to take.

When the word 'seed' or the concept of planting a seed is used in the Bible it is an alliteration for thought. Galatians' 6:7 is a perfect example; *"Whatever a man sows, that shall he also reap."* If we plant carrots, we will get carrots, not potatoes, or beans. The carrot seed knows how to become a carrot. It needs planting in fertile soil, water, sunshine, time to grow, and freedom from being choked by weeds.

So it is with our prayers. In treatment we plant the thought (the seed). Now it needs to be nourished, nurtured, and kept free of interference (the weeds). Any action we take after

---

treatment can be likened to caring for the garden. Beliefs and habits are connected. Treatment changes beliefs. Changing beliefs changes habits. Making a conscious effort to change our habits' speeds and assists the change in beliefs. Our beliefs are deeply rooted within us; changing a belief can take both time and energy.

In the Epistle of James we find the following. *"Faith without works is dead. I will show you my faith by my works. By his works, his faith was made perfect."* James 2:17-18, 22. The work that we do, the actions that we take must complement the new belief that is replacing the old belief.

Our lives represent a trinity that includes the physical, mental and spiritual. A Spiritual Mind Treatment is a mental activity of the conscious (objective) mind directed to the universal (subjective) mind. Any additional action that we take, whether mental or physical, prepares us to accept the result of the treatment.

There are a number of positive actions that can be taken to assist the treatment in transforming a life from the old limiting belief into an expanded level of consciousness. Some are very simple and take almost no time at all. Others are considerably more active; requiring a greater commitment in time, energy, and effort. Whether, with a particular issue in your life, you use one or all of these actions depends on how great the challenge is and how committed you are to correcting it. The following activities give an introduction and basic information on actions that can be taken after treatment.

Reading

The very fact that you picked up this book and have read this far is a positive step in your spiritual growth. However, reading alone is a passive activity. If you have not stopped and written a treatment for yourself yet, do so! It is too easy to read a book, say, "That's nice," and start to read another book. Yet, reading is an important way to acquire knowledge. Any subject that one is interested in will have an entire section devoted to it in the local library. Experts in any particular field who have devoted their lives to the subject have written more books than we have time to read. There is a short suggested reading list in the back of this book, but it is only a place to begin, not a complete inventory of books available. There is an enormous variety of books written on health issues, abundance, prosperity, and relationships. There are books on affirmations, visualizations, forgiveness, etc.

Affirming

Belief systems are hidden deep within the subconscious mind. An affirmation is a positive statement that is repeated to assist the objective mind in reprogramming the subjective mind. **We are always doing affirmations!** Listen to the conversation that goes on within your head. Do you hear yourself say, "I'll never..." or "I can't..." or "I always..." These are affirmations. Are you affirming the ideas you want to be true in your life? Or are you affirming the limiting beliefs that you have accepted for yourself. Limiting beliefs can be changed! Become aware of them, write them down, and then create some new positive affirmations to change the old beliefs.

A little more mental activity is required to create and repeat affirmations than to sit and read, but these are positive and effective activities. Short easily remembered affirmations are preferred.

The rules for creating a positive affirmation are similar to the instructions for the third or affirmation step described in chapter five: keep it short, keep it positive, and in present time. Write the affirmation on a 3x5 index card or a scrap of paper and keep it in your pocket where it can be retrieved and read any time of day or memorize it. A good time to repeat affirmations is when walking, waiting in line, driving, or any time when you begin to worry or fear.

Here is a short list of affirmations to use as thought stimulators to create your own:

God's healing energy flows through my body.

My life is abundant and prosperous.

I see love, peace, and harmony wherever I look.

Divine Love surrounds me.

Spirit is the Source of all my good.

Divine Guidance directs my life.

All the knowledge in Universal Mind is available to me.

The safety, peace, and calm of Spirit protects me.

This moment is filled with Divine right action.

Visualizing

It takes time and concentration to create a visualization exercise. However, it can be even more powerful than an affirmation. Use the creative power of imagination to picture the result you want as if you already have it. It may help to pretend you are in a movie theater projecting images on the screen. I recommend that you find a place where it is quiet, where you can be alone and undisturbed for a short time. Sit in a chair that supports your back completely and comfortably. Place your feet flat on the floor. Put your hands in your lap with palms up and form a circle with the thumb and index finger. Take a few deep breaths to relax. If there is any tension or discomfort in your body, tense and then relax the muscles surrounding that area.

Here are a few sample visualizations to begin with:

For general relaxation: Picture yourself in a peaceful nature setting. It may be a mountain, meadow, seashore, or forest. Imagine that you are completely calm, safe, and at peace with the environment. Hear the sounds of birds singing, waves lapping upon the shore, or breeze whistling through the trees. Feel the warmth of the sun or coolness of the shade. Smell the sweet odors of nature surrounding you. Notice that in God's nature there is a sense of peace.

For a sense of connection with Spirit: Imagine a bright pure white light far above you shining down on the top of your head. Picture that light expanding and surrounding your body like a stage spotlight. Know that this light is God's love surrounding and supporting you at all times.

For a thing that you want, whether a computer, a car or a kitten: Picture it in every detail. Imagine yourself working with it, playing with it, enjoying it.

For a healing in a part of the body: Imagine a beautiful flower right in the middle of your chest by your heart. See that flower blossom and open. Picture a soft green light coming out of that flower, surrounding your body completely. Now see the light glowing brightly right in the spot where the healing is to take place. As you inhale, picture the afflicted area absorbing the healing green light. As you exhale picture the pain and disease moving out of the body and being released.

For abundance: Picture nature's abundance: countless grains of sand on a beach, leaves on a tree, blades of grass on a large lawn, snowflakes in a winter storm. Imagine dollar bills gently falling all around you. Know that God's abundance is as freely given as the snowflakes.

Forgiving

Sometimes we find that we need to free ourselves from the hurtful effects of another person by releasing the negative thoughts about that person. These negative thoughts can be released through forgiveness. It is vitally important to do the work necessary to release. Sometimes we need to forgive the errors of the past done by others and sometimes we need to forgive our own errors that restrain our forward progress. *Radical Forgiveness* by Colin Tipping is an excellent book on this topic.

Getting professional help

Is professional counseling needed? It may be time to see a doctor, nutritional counselor, masseuse, debt counselor, payer practitioner, pastor, or therapist. For those with addictions, it may be time to join a twelve-step group and work the steps. When we know in our heart that we need professional help, and we deny ourselves that help, we are only making a bad situation worse.

Once professional expertise is sought, the next step seems obvious. Follow the steps, take the medicine, change the diet, get the rest or exercise needed. Do what is recommended. Do what the professional advises. It is amazing to me how many times expensive medical advice is ignored. I had a dear friend who died of lung cancer. Despite several operations, spitting up blood daily, and not being able to speak a sentence without a hacking cough, she continued to smoke until it killed her. Another friend, in the hospital supposedly recovering from a heart attack was on the telephone screaming at a supplier to his business. Heart problems are healed by love not conflict.

Weeding the Garden

One of the most important actions that we have to take for any issue is what I will call "weeding." This is removing the weeds from the garden that can strangle the new plants, or the new beliefs. These weeds are usually old thought patterns. They are voices inside our heads. It is important to become aware of what we say to our self. These voices may be feeding us negative affirmations and need to be replaced immediately and persistently with positive affirmations that override them and lift your mind toward the new belief system that is being changed through treatment. The good news is that as we start to pray for changes, we become more aware of the negative voices and more able to root them out.

We need to be continually vigilant. It is important to be aware of the negativity that we accept. In the normal course of our daily routine we are continually bombarded by negativity. Most news programs are negative. Even if they have something positive to report they put a negative cast on it. Commercials are designed to make us feel insecure and ineffective. They tell us that if we buy the product offered then we will be all right. Other people around us may have accepted negativity into their own lives. It is a constant process to be aware of this negative input and refuse to accept it. If we do not continually weed the garden, deciding for ourselves which seeds (thoughts) we allow to grow there, we are accepting other people's negativity.

Dag Hammarskjold said, *"No one should reserve a corner of his mind or his garden for weeds. For once they are started there is no stopping them."* Unfortunately, we already have a corner of weeds in the garden of our mind. A gardener carefully plucks out the weeds and replaces them with the seeds of his desired harvest. So we can create a prayer to replace the erroneous belief system with the belief that fully serves us.

Attending Seminars and Workshops

A seminar, workshop, or retreat can be a life-changing event. This is an opportunity in a highly concentrated form, usually over a weekend, to work through some of the issues that are affecting our life.

Suggested Activities for Abundance, Health and Relationships

The following exercises are only suggestions. Be creative. Make up our own. These are just ideas to assist your thinking in what might be the best for you.

Abundance

Let's say that you have prayed for abundance. In order to reinforce the new belief that you deserve more of what you want it is often good to take stock of what you have. Notice how much you have received, how much abundance is already in your life. Make a list. Take a note pad and go around your home and write down all the things you own. Thank God for each one and bless it. Appreciating and thanking the Source of All for what you have can effect a great change in your attitude toward abundance and your belief in what you deserve. Obviously you deserve everything that you have. Bless it and more will flow.

Another activity that is an important part of the abundance issue is noticing the way we take care of what money we have. Money that is thrown away or misspent is like seeds thrown in a river. They may take root and grow someday, but too far downstream to benefit the farmer who might have planted them more thoughtfully.

By starting a savings program and saving even as little as twenty dollars a week and noticing the growth of that savings, you begin a new habit which reinforces the belief in abundance.

Sharing some of your income also establishes a belief in abundance. A routine donation program, whether a tithe to your church, a weekly gift to a charity, or simply the habit of tossing your shopping change into a charity collection box is an action that shows your belief in the prayer for abundance. If there is resistance to a donation or a savings plan, it is an indication that more work needs to be done on your belief. *"Give and it will be given unto you,"* Luke 6:38.

Sometimes we need to clear out, let go, and throw away the old to make room for the new to come into our lives. Are you praying for a new wardrobe? Clean out the old and give away anything that you have not worn in the last year. Are you praying for a new car? Advertise your old one for sale. Do you wish a new place to live? Get the weekend paper and go look. Do you desire a new, exciting career? Take a class. Talk to people in that field. Read the trade magazines. Take at least one action to support the new belief.

Health
We are incredibly fortunate to live in a world so abundant and prosperous that we each choose how we are going to live in it. Such a wonderful diversity of opportunities is avail-

able that we suffer from the stress of sampling too many. There is an incredible variety of choices in the food we eat from the healthiest fresh vegetables to the greasiest donuts. A wide variety of employment is available and new careers are being created every day. There are more types of entertainment, hobbies and leisure activities than we could ever pursue. We often get so busy that we do not take the time for exercise, meditation, contemplation, and rest.

An illness is a wake up call, a cry from the body for help. It can be an opportunity to make better choices to extend and fulfill our lives. A health issue may have a corresponding belief behind it and an action that can be taken along with treatment to change the belief. Here are a few specific health challenges followed by an underlying belief that may cause them. For more information on this subject see Louise Hays book, *"You Can Heal Your Life."* (See suggested Readings.)

Sore throat? Is there something that you should say to someone? Are you holding in your anger? You may have to express your feelings, or apologize or make amends for something you did.

Ear trouble? There may be a message that you do not want to hear. Many of life's "surprises" were quite predictable. Quite often we were told exactly what was going to happen, but were not listening.

Headache? Are you afraid of something? Have you been self-critical? Is the voice in your head telling you that you are wrong?

Colds (upper-respiratory illness)? Are you confused, working three jobs, dating three people, making promises and commitments that you believe cannot possibly be fulfilled? Is your home and car cluttered with useless trash? Do you believe it has to be that way? Or is it time to clean up, say no, cut back, or slow down.

Relationship

If there is a challenge in a relationship, be aware of your part in the interactions that take place. Is there a subject that needs to be discussed that has been hidden? Are you too busy to have a discussion? Are your own issues so important in your mind that you are being inconsiderate of the feelings of others? Ego and righteousness often interfere with healthy relationships. We are all humans doing the best we can. Sometimes an honest conversation is enough to begin the healing of the most seemingly insurmountable difficulties.

If you have no relationship, fear of intimacy may be an issue. Join a group in which you have an interest that attracts people of both genders, such as hiking or skiing, a charitable organization, a hobby guild, a professional association, or Toastmasters group. Take a class. Join a single's group. Volunteer at a local museum. Go with the intention of making friends rather than finding "the perfect mate." Take a small step today that will put you into interaction with members of the opposite gender in a way in which you feel safe and comfortable.

Releasing the dead wood

There is often a need to release an issue that is consistently on your mind and affecting all other activities. Here is an outrageous idea. Write the problem on a block of scrap wood. For example you might write "Father's abuse," "Bosses' meanness," "Husband's anger," "Headaches," "Belief in lack of money," on a scrap of wood. Then tie a long string around the wood and tie it to your waist and drag it around with you for a while. When you are tired of dragging it, take a pair of scissors and cut the string with the Affirmation, "I cut you loose. Good-bye!"

CHAPTER ELEVEN

TREATING FOR OTHERS

Treating for another person is a privilege and a responsibility. It is in some ways easier and in some ways more difficult than praying for oneself. Easier because we are normally more capable of seeing the image of God's perfection in another person than in ourselves. It may be easier to get a clear picture of the underlying issue and belief that affects another's life. Our own issues are often so clouded in our own history, buried by denial and low self-esteem, that it is difficult to honestly and rationally face them.

There is one word of caution concerning praying for another person. Do not pray for anyone who does not specifically ask for prayer. It is presumptuous to assume that we know when or how to pray for another person without the active participation or permission of that person. Assume someone asks me to pray for his brother. He tells me that his brother is a Republican. All of the family members for three generations have been Democrats so he believes something must be wrong with his brother. This is an amusing, obvious, and ridiculous example. However, suppose the same person came to me because his brother has cancer and he wants his brother to be cured. Perhaps he has a higher motive, but it is just as intrusive in his brother's life. Does the brother want to be cured? Louise Hay has cured herself and many others of cancer. In her book, *"You Can Heal Your Life,"* she says that cancer can be caused by deep hurt and grief, and carrying hatreds and resentments. It is one of the many diseases imposed upon the body by the mind. To be cured of cancer the brother may need to let go of resentments or hatreds or whatever is the cause of the mental condition, which has led to his illness. Only he can determine whether or not he is ready to seek the change needed for healing.

One of the most frequent requests for prayers for a family member has to do with alcohol or drug addictions. If you speak to the addict he will deny that he has a problem, and may even blame his troubles on the meddler who asked you to pray. When the addict or the cancer victim comes and asks for prayer for him/her self, that person is ready to accept, deal with, and change the situation. Then prayer will be in harmony rather than in conflict with the desires of the person for whom the prayer is done.

One way to handle a person who wants you to pray for another is to discuss how that individual is affected by the other's actions. If Patrick wishes me to pray for Phil, I ask how Phil's cancer, alcoholism, Democratism or whatever affects Patrick. What are Patrick's feelings, fears, and anxieties? What are Patrick's beliefs that are challenged? Perhaps we write a treatment for Patrick to realize love, understanding, and acceptance.

When someone asks us to pray for them we must be aware that we do the prayer work within our own mind. Remember that all minds are connected within the Universal Mind of Spirit. We see and accept the spiritual perfection of the one for whom we pray. We are not convincing them, or asking God to change them. They are already perfect in the eyes of God.

Before doing a prayer for someone else it is important to listen carefully to what they have to say about the condition for which they are requesting prayer. Along with helping to clarify the purpose of the prayer, listening carefully has benefits for the person in pain. As they speak, they will release a great deal of the intensity of emotions that are temporarily limiting their ability to think clearly. This gives them an opportunity to express and clarify what may have been vague, often undefined feelings. We listen to understand, not to find a solution, fix a problem or give advice.

There is a great value in having a receptive, quiet listener to share our pain. We are often taught to keep our trouble or confusion to ourselves. Repressing the discomfort or pain can cause damage to our body or mind. When seeking comfort or understanding from others we may get responses like, "Everybody's got problems, Pal," or "You think that's bad, let me tell you what happened to me." This does not benefit the person seeking help. Non-judgmental listening will allow that person to release their feelings and express him/her self more clearly. It is not unusual to find that by simply expressing the problem clearly they gain a new valuable insight into their own participation in the drama.

If possible, I like to ask some probing questions to clarify the situation in my own mind. I also need to remember that they themselves may not be consciously clear about the underlying belief that is causing their current pain. Although each situation is unique, here are some questions that I find myself commonly asking:

Exactly what happened?

Has this ever happened before?

Why do you think that this happened?

How has it affected you?

What is your part in it?

Specifically, what do you want me to pray for?

Usually the answers to these questions give me a clear picture of the belief behind the challenge or lead to further questions that will help me understand. Often I will pray for exactly what they ask for. In any event, I do not begin a treatment until I get the individuals approval for the purpose of the prayer. Sometimes they do not have a specific purpose. Then I ask, "May I pray for Divine Right Action to take place in your life?" In the Bible verse immediately before the Lord's Prayer we read, *"Your Father knows what you need, before you ask him."* (Matthew 6:8).

After I pray for another, I will often write a prescription. If the word prescription offends you, consider it homework (see chapter ten, Taking Action). A medical doctor friend, in a surprising display of candor, once told me that a high percentage of his patients do not really need a prescription for their dis-ease. However, most people feel incomplete leaving a medical office without one! The purpose of the prescription or homework is to add a physical element to the prayer. Since prayer treatment is an example of the objective or conscious mind working to change a situation or condition, adding a physical element increases the effectiveness of the prayer. A prescription I suggest may be an affirmation, an exercise, visualization, suggestion to write their own treatment, or something else that comes to mind through any insight gathered during our discussion. Take for example, a person, feeling lack and limitation, for whom I have created a treatment for abundance. I may prescribe that they take a yellow pad and go through each room in their house listing and appreciating the abundance they already have.

For a person feeling loneliness, who has asked for a prayer for a significant relationship I might suggest that every time they pass a mirror, they stop, look directly into their own eyes, and say, "I love you."

The following are two examples of situations for which someone asked me to do treatment, followed by the prayer that was done and a suggested prescription.

Example of prayer to release a cold:

Pat had a cold and wanted me to pray to get rid of the symptoms. During our discussion she told me that she gets a cold every February. She also said that her life was very busy. Her job was demanding, her family was challenging, she had been taking a night class and involved in many other activities. All of this busy-ness caused mental confusion, which is one of the prime causes of colds. I suggested a treatment for peace, love, and calmness, knowing that all of her activities meld harmoniously together and that she moves easily and peacefully from one to the other. For action after prayer I suggested that she make sure all of the activities she was involved with served her. Were there tasks imposed upon her by others? Were there some that she did not want to do? Can she say, "No"?

When praying for others we speak the first two steps of Spiritual Mind Treatment just as if we were treating for ourselves. Then I include the other person with what is called a "segue." Segue is a musical term meaning to proceed without pause. Broadcasters use the term to describe the linkage of one subject with another. The form I use is normally written like this: "As this is true for me it is also true for ____."

Although I may then use the other persons name in the third step, it is still my treatment. I might say, "I know that ____ is perfect." In the fourth step I express my gratitude for the privilege of praying for that person.

The fifth step is release, letting go, allowing the treatment its own life. This is particularly important when treating for others. We need to be sure that we let it go, forget it, know that it is complete. We do not take the burden of their issues upon ourselves. We do not call them later to ask how the prayer worked, or if it worked, or if their lives are wonderfully transformed because of it. Let it go. It is complete. If they should return another time and ask for another prayer, that is a new treatment with its own purpose, words, and action.

Example of a prayer to release Pat's cold:

Recognition: The Universe exists as Perfect Health. The Mind of Creative Spirit is alive, vital, complete at all times. Within God all is peace, harmony, calm.

Unification: I celebrate my connection with the Spirit of peace. I am surrounded at all times by gracious harmony. My life is a calm demonstration of God's love.

Segue: As this is true for me, it is also true for Pat.

Affirmation: I know that right now she is an expression of God walking on this earth. That in every moment the love of Nature surrounds her and brings her peace. All of the elements of Pat's life are dealt with in their own time and according to their own importance. All of her activities support her good. Each moment brings her joy. Her mind is calm. Her relationships are harmonious. Her days are filled with vital, joyous adventures.

I am grateful today for the peace and harmony that exists in my life, for the joy that knowing life is in harmony with Spirit.

I release this treatment into the loving Mind of Creative Energy, knowing that it is complete. And so it is.

Prescription for Pat: Stop whatever you are doing, sit comfortably in a chair with your feet flat on the floor, back
straight, eyes closed, and your hands in your lap.
Breathe in deeply and slowly, hold it for a few seconds,
and then let it out slowly. Dosage: Ten deep breaths at
every attack of coughing or sneezing.

Example of a prayer to heal a relationship:

Joanne came to me with a relationship challenge with
one of her coworkers. She requested a prayer that the coworker
quit or be transferred or leave in some fashion. The language
Joanne used to describe her coworker was amazingly colorful.
Let's just report that they argued often. As we talked, it became
apparent that there was simply a personality conflict between
two people who both cared about doing a capable job for their
employer, but had differing ideas as to how that was to be accomplished.

I cannot, must not pray to affect a third person who is
not a party to this request, who has not asked for treatment. I
pray to know in my own mind, which is inseparably connected
with the Divine Mind, the spiritual perfection of Joanne.

What I learned from our discussion was that Joanne
liked her job and had been doing it alone for several years. As
the company grew, the job expanded until one person could not
handle it. The coworker, a long time company employee, did
not want to be moved into that job. Joanne looked upon her as
more interference than help.

Example of prayer for peace and harmony on the job for
Joanne:

Recognition: There is a Power of Divine Love that encompasses the world. This Love reaches every corner of the globe inspiring peace and harmony at all times.

Unification: That Higher Power continually influences my mind. My connection with Divine Love brings peace and harmony to every moment of my life.

Segue: As this is true for me it is also true for Joanne.

Affirmation: At this moment I know that Joanne is surrounded by peace, harmony and love. I know that throughout the working day she is calm, efficiently performing her tasks to the best of her abilities. As she continues with her work nothing can penetrate this Divine atmosphere of peace. The Spirit of Love carries her through every situation, every discussion, and every moment. Harmony prevails and joy lifts her heart.

Gratitude: Gratitude touches me with the knowledge of the peace, harmony and love surrounding Joanne's working environment.

Release: Peacefully, graciously, I release this treatment to the harmony of Divine Love. Amen.

Prescription for Joanne: Take a deep breath. Understand that this coworker is not mad at Joanne but at herself. Mentally send a cloud of pure white light filled with God's love to surround that person. Smile and say, "Thank you." Dosage: Do this each time the coworker speaks out in anger.

There are people who are trained, accredited and licensed to give Spiritual Mind Treatments.   There are also churches, study groups and education centers that teach the techniques that I have outlined here.   Lists of them will be found in the back pages of *Science of Mind Magazine* and *Creative Thought Magazine*.   See the "Suggested Readings" section at the back of this book for their address and web site.

CHAPTER TWELVE

THE TREATMENT DIDN'T WORK?

"In the Beginning was the Word, and the Word was with God, and the Word was God." (John 1:1).

Treatment always works. We speak our word using our objective mind (intellect), working through the Natural Law (Divine Mind) to reprogram the beliefs held in our subjective mind. Every treatment has an effect on the subjective mind. If it does not seem to work quickly enough for us, it may be that the old belief is so thoroughly ingrained that it will take more than one attempt to change it. Like a garden full of weeds, we clear them out and some grow back. We clear them again and some grow back. Fewer grow back each time until finally they are under control and the flowers and vegetables can flourish.

I pray for myself every day. In most cases my prayers are simple treatments for a successful day. I pray for God's words to flow through my brain and fingers unto the keyboard and into my computer. I pray that I will have a safe trip if I am traveling. I pray for clarity of my message if I am teaching. I pray that I enjoy a peaceful night's sleep. When I am dealing with a serious issue that persists, I often ask someone else to pray for me as I may be too close to my own problems. I may be tied to the old belief because it served me in the past. I am also stubborn, resistant, and lazy, especially if it means that I have to make a change in my life. However, eventually the pain becomes unbearable. I go to someone who asks me the same questions that I ask others, creates a treatment for me that I use to change my belief, and possibly even gives me a prescription to support the treatment.

When it appears that a treatment is not working, there are some possibilities to explore. It is not the prayer itself, or the words. There are no magic words. No bad words, no bad treatments. We may make a few technical errors but they are rarely the problem. The Source of Universal Love is very forgiving. This Source does not pounce like a prosecuting attorney on every misspoken word.

Let's look at technical errors first and then move on to the more likely challenges. If the treatment was strictly oral, it is complete, done, and forgotten. So it cannot be analyzed. This is one reason that I like written treatments and strongly suggest that while learning, all treatments are written. The first place to consider is the Unification step. I know that I am an expression of God's Love in human form and cannot be disconnected from that Source, yet there are times in the busy-ness of my life, that I feel estranged. This is a time to put down the pencil, sit quietly and visualize that Divine Love is surrounding me. I picture a beam of pure white light coming down from way above and surrounding me like a spotlight on a stage.

The second place to look for a possible technical error would be in the Realization Step. Is it written in a positive manner? If you say, "I have no limitations," you are speaking in what writers call, "the negative voice." Do not reverse your message with a negative; speak affirmatively. Say instead, "I am unlimited!"

Affirm that what you want you already have in the present. God only works in present time; now is the only time that exists. If you write in future tense, saying, "I **will** have...(money, relationships, health, or whatever)" it is an indication that you don't want it now.

The third technical error that can crop up is in the fifth step. Did you really release the treatment or have you kept dragging it back and reworking it? Release means forgiveness and acceptance. Forget it. Let go! Move on.

A more likely problem than any wording or phraseology in the actual prayer itself is in the action or lack of it taken after the prayer is released. We can pray for new employment, but we need to make ourselves available to employers by sending out resumes, and filling out applications. If we treat for a special relationship and stay locked in our room where nobody can find us, the results may be disappointing. If we are dissatisfied with our health and continue to smoke, drink, and feed on donuts and potato chips, we should not be surprised if we stay sick.

The most likely challenge to successful demonstration of a treatment has to do with the beliefs that we want to affect. First consider the belief system of the person doing the treatment. For example: suppose someone came to me with an amputated leg and asked me to pray that a new one would grow. I do believe in miracles but I do not believe that anyone can grow a new leg. This means that I cannot treat that issue for that person. Perhaps someone who has a greater belief than I could do it. I could discuss the grief process with him and write a prayer to help him deal with the denial, anger, guilt, and fear that is a part of any loss. I can treat for him to work through that grief process and eventually come to acceptance of the loss. I can treat to look past the loss and begin to build a new life or find whatever benefit the experience holds. I can treat for myself to expand my belief and to help him find comfort.

It is vitally important that we seek to understand the belief systems operating in the person who asks for the treatment. Suppose someone comes in to request a treatment to win the lottery. This person says that they are desperate. Out of work, again. Broke, again. He is unable to pay the rent, again. He sees the lottery as the answer to all of his problems. There are numerous examples of people with a belief in lack and poverty who have come into large sums of money. Then, because they did not believe they deserved money, they threw it away and wound up broke again. If we simply treat to win the lottery, we will most likely be disappointed. However, by understanding the belief he holds about money, we may find that we can pray successfully for gainful, steady employment, or for a change in his belief in lack, limitation, and poverty to a belief in abundance and prosperity.

We most often find that peoples' beliefs are tied to low self-esteem, a feeling of unworthiness. If we have not determined the root issue, the underlying belief that is holding them back, we are most likely treating for the wrong situation. Sometimes through guilt, shame, or embarrassment they will not tell us. Then we can treat for clarity, for divine right action in their lives, for the knowledge that they are an expression of God on earth, and that they deserve to have abundance, health, loving relationships.

If someone returns for a new prayer concerning the same issue, probe more deeply into the belief system and the manifestations of a person's life that support it. Some beliefs are obvious. Some are not. The following are some examples of probing deeper into the cause and making changes that worked:

Casey came to me for a treatment for non-clinical depression. We talked. I prayed. He left. Two weeks later he called to tell me that although he felt better for a couple of days, he was right back into such deep depression that it was affecting his job. When we got together again I asked him to describe his day. Among other things he told me was that he listened to the morning news on television before going to work, the evening news after work, the 11:00 pm news before going to bed. Since he did a lot of driving during the day, his truck radio was tuned to an all news station.

We decided that perhaps he could stay sufficiently informed with only one newscast each day and he chose the 6:00 pm news after work. During the 7:00 am news time and the 11:00 pm news time he would write a treatment for peace and harmony in the world. He decided to change the station on his truck radio to one that played soothing, gentle music. During the hourly newsbreaks he would shut off the radio and spend the five minutes looking for signs of peace and harmony. It might be two men talking quietly together, a couple holding hands, a woman playing with her child. Then I did a treatment to the effect that Casey was surrounded by peace, harmony, and joy every day. I saw him a week later, smiling, whistling, standing tall, his face bright and happy. He told me prayer works.

Linda had a series of colds all winter. Several people had treated for her. After each prayer she felt better. Later she would catch another cold. As a schoolteacher, she blamed it on her students, it seemed as though one or the other always had a cold. After the treatment was complete I walked her out to her car. I noticed the back seat was filled with junk. It contained pieces of school projects, poster paper, crayons, and newspapers. The front seat was filled with books. The floor held foam coffee cups and lunch bags from fast food chains. We discussed the clutter within the car and I asked if her home was in similar disarray. She claimed her house made the car look almost neat.

For her homework I suggested an hour each day of what I called clearing out the congestion. The first day she was to clear anything out of her car that did not pertain to the operation of the vehicle. Then she would clean one section of her house each day. Do a room one day, a closet the next. Throw away, store, file, return, or recycle. When the car was empty, I suggested she have it professionally cleaned and polished. When the house was neat I suggested she have a cleaning person come in to wash windows, bathrooms, kitchen, etc.

A week later I saw Linda in church. She had a new dress and a new hairdo. Her face sparkled. She sparkled. She told me that she had invited some friends in to help her clean house and gotten it all done in one day. Her cold went out with the trash. Releasing a belief in confusion and clutter is not easy. But it can change a life.

There are those people who pray for a certain thing that does not occur. During the process they realize that what they have been praying for is not what they really want. It seems as though it would be good to have more money, because the world appears to relate money and the things it can buy to happiness. It seems as though it would be a good idea to be younger, stronger, more slender, better looking. This is because the people on television commercials who seem to have such wonderful fun filled lives look that way. It seems as though it would be good to have more fulfilling relationships, more laughter, love, sex, excitement, because the people in the romance novels have it that way.

As we are first learning spiritual Mind Treatment, many of our prayers are for the purpose of changing the outward effects of our lives. However, the result of spiritual mind treatment is a change in an internal belief. All of our current belief systems serve us in some way. That is why we keep them and hold on to them so strongly.

As we learn and practice spiritual mind treatment we find a shift occurs somewhere deep within us. This is a shift from the physical or intellectual to the spiritual level. It is a transformation where we begin understand that we are spiritual beings having a human experience. We begin to have a greater love and acceptance of ourselves as we have created our lives, and understand that we are the way God expresses here on earth. We understand that the Source that created the Universe is within us and is constantly recreating us. We know that we are one with that Spirit and with all of its expressions walking on the planet. We realize the truth of the statement, *"Behold, the Kingdom of God is within you,"* (Luke 17:21).

As a shift occurs, our treatments shift as well. We treat less for physical effects and more for spiritual enlightenment. Correspondingly, as we grow and develop, our treatments on the physical level demonstrate more effectively, sometimes beyond anything we could imagine. Then we can truly understand the statement of Jesus during his Sermon on the Mount, *"Seek first the Kingdom of God, and all these things shall be added unto you,"* (Matthew 6:33).

NAMASTE

SUGGESTED READINGS

BOOKS

Addington, Jack. *The Perfect Power Within You.* DeVorss 1973

Butterworth, Eric. *Spritual Economics.* Unity House 2001

Chopra, Deepak. *The Path to Love.* Harmony Books 1997

Cohen, Alan. *A Deep Breath of Life.* Hay House 1976

Dreamer, Oriah Mountain. *The Dance.* Harper 2001

Emerson, Ralph Waldo. *Essays and Lectures.* Literary Classics 1983

Fox, Emmet. *Sermon on the Mount.* Harper Collins 1934

Fox, Matthew. *One River, Many Wells.* Tarcher/Putnam 2000

Gibran, Kahlil. *The Prophet.* Alfred A Knopf 1923

Grayson, Stewart. *Spiritual Healing.* Simon & Schuster 1997

Han, Thich Nhat. *Teaching on Love.* Parallax Press 1998

Hay, Louise. *You Can Heal Your Life.* Hay House, 1987

Holmes, Ernest. *The Science of Mind*. Penguin Putnam, 1938

Kornfield, Jack. *After the Ectasy, the Laundry.* Bantam 2000

Ruiz, don Miguel. *The Four Agreements.* Amber-Allen 1998

Tipping, Colin C. *Radical Forgiveness.* Global 13 Publications

Tolle, Eckhart. *The Power of Now.* New World Library 1999

Troward, Thomas. *The Edinburgh Lectures.* DeVorss. 1989

Venzant, Iyanla. *One Day My Heart Just Opened Up.* Fireside 1988

Walsh, Neale Donald. *Conversations With God.* Hampton Roads. 1998

Williamson, Marianne. *The Healing of America.* Simon & Schuster 1997

Zukav, Gary. *The Seat of the Soul.* Fireside 1989

MAGAZINES

Creative Thought
P.O. Box 2152
Spokane Washington 99210
www.rsintl.org
(800) 662-1348

Science of Mind
P.O. Box 75127
Los Angeles, CA 09975
www.scienceofmind.com
(800) 247-6463

Available in Borders Books

BIBLE QUOTES

I have used three different Bibles. The King James Version, which is the most poetic; The American Standard Version, which is today's best selling Bible; and the George Lamsa Bible, which is the most accurate translation from ancient manuscripts, (Holman Bible Publishers, Nashville). The particular quotations used reflect my own opinion of which seemed better suited to the text. In every case I suggest that you compare to your own Bible, reading not just the verse quoted but the context in which it appears.

Peter C. Gray has had a varied and interesting career. He writes, creates photographs and sells real estate in Morris County, New Jersey. You can contact him through E-mail at petegray@inpro.net.